CIGARS

NEIL MILLINGTON

SELECT
EDITIONS

This edition first published in 1998 by
PRC Publishing Ltd,
Kiln House, 210 New Kings Road, London SW6 4NZ
exclusively for Selecta Book Ltd, Folly Road, Roundway, Devizes,
Wiltshire SN10 2hr

Copyright © 1998 PRC Publishing Ltd.

ISBN 1 85648 454 8

Printed and bound in China

This book has been written in association with Havana
Club, 165 Sloane Street, London SW1X 9QB, renowned
for a huge selection of fine cigars. Havana Club can be
contacted on 44 (0)171 245 0890 (phone); 44 (0)171 245
0895 (fax).

Acknowledgements
I should like to thank all those at Monte's Club on
Sloane Street, without whose patience this book would
not have transpired. Next Hunters & Frankau, the sole
importers of Havana Cigars in the UK, must be thanked
for their continuing support and supply of some great
smokes and for helping with illustrations. Richard and
Maritza Ulrych of Valdrych Cigars Ltd. also need to be
thanked for "insider information" on Dominican cigars.
Toby Brocklehurst from Special Places must be thanked
too for his company's organisation of cigar tours to
Cuba, which I was fortunate enough to be invited on.
The week spent in Cuba has given me a great insight
into the manufacturing processes of some of the world's
finest cigars. Lastly, I need to thank my sister, Deborah,
without whose typing skills I could not have managed.

Previous page: A Vegas Robaina Don Alejandro.
Below: A Havana Club humidor.

Preface

Over the past five or so years there has been a huge renaissance in the cigar world, mainly in the United States, but also in the Far East and to a lesser extent Europe.

Cigar smoking has received massive publicity with the launch of several magazines dedicated to the cigar, notably *Cigar Aficionado* owned by Marvin Shanken, an American "bon viveur" with a passion for the finer things in life, especially cigars. Hollywood has grasped the trend with both hands; stars such as Arnold Schwarzenegger, Danny DeVito, and James Woods have all graced the cover of *Cigar Aficionado*. Cigar smoking—always seen to be a male dominated domain—is now proving popular with the fairer sex: Madonna, Glenn Close, Demi Moore, and Claudia Schiffer are all cigar smokers and it would seem that women

have broken down one of the last bastions of maleness and enjoy smoking fine cigars as much as men do.

This book has been written with the new cigar smoker in mind and I have tried to keep the terminology as simple as possible so as not to confuse the inexperienced smoker. I hope you will enjoy your journey through the world of cigars as much as I have over the last ten years.

Neil Millington
Havana Club
November
1997

Glossary

8-9-8 box	type of cigar box, containing 25 cigars
Belvederes	5in. long cigar with a ring gauge of 39
bunch	semi-finished cigar, when the leaves are collected together ready for rolling
burros	pile of fermenting leaves
cabinet	type of cigar box
Cadete	4½in. long cigar with a ring gauge of 36
café	Also called English market selection, or natural. Light brown wrapper is usual for Connecticut shade tobacco
Campana	5½in. long cigar with a ring gauge of 52
candella	cigars with a pale green wrapper
cap	end of the cigar, attached with gum
capa	wrapper
capote	binder
Carolina	4¾in. long cigar with a ring gauge of 26
Casas del Tabaco	tobacco curing barn
Cervante	6½in. long cigar with a ring gauge of 42
chaveta	a flat blade, the only tool in hand-made cigar making
Chicos	4⅛in. long cigar with a ring gauge of 29
Claro	one of the main shades of cigar
Colorado	one of the main shades of cigar
Colorado claro	one of the main shades of cigar
Corojo	type of tobacco plant
Corona	5½in. long cigar with a ring gauge of 42
Corona gorda	5⅝in. long cigar with a ring gauge of 46
Corona grande	6⅛in. long cigar with a ring gauge of 42
Criollo	type of tobacco plant
Dalia	6¾in. long cigar with a ring gauge of 43
Entreacto	3⅞in. long cigar with a ring gauge of 30
Escaparate	conditioning room
Escogida	color grading room
figurado	specialized cigar shape, with pointed tips and non-parallel sides
flat box	type of cigar box
Franciscano	4½in. long cigar with a ring

	gauge of 40
Gran corona	9¼in. long cigar with a ring gauge of 47
guillotine	used to trim the cigar
H.T.L.	Homogenized Tobacco Leaf.
Heavy gauge	has a ring gauge between 45 and 52
Hecho en Cuba	made in Cuba
Hermoso No. 4	5in. long cigar with a ring gauge of 48
Julieta	7in. long cigar with a ring gauge of 48
Laguito No. 1	7½in. long cigar with a ring gauge of 38
Laguito No. 2	6in. long cigar with a ring gauge of 38
Laguito No. 3	4½in. long cigar with a ring gauge of 26
ligero	the top tobacco leaves
Maduro	one of the main shades of cigar
Mareva	5in. long cigar with a ring gauge of 42
medias ruedas	bundles of 50 cigars
Minuto	4⅜in. long cigar with a ring gauge of 42
Nacionales	5½in. long cigar with a ring gauge of 40
Ninfas	7in. long cigar with a ring gauge of 33
oscuro	almost black cigars
Perla	4in. long cigar with a ring gauge of 40
Petit Cetro	5in. long cigar with a ring gauge of 40
Prominente	7⅞in. long cigar with a ring gauge of 49
Pyramide	6⅛in. long cigar with a ring gauge of 52
ring gauge	diameter of a cigar measured in 64ths of an inch
Robusto	4⅞in. long cigar with a ring gauge of 50
S.B.N.	semi-boîte nature, cigar box
seco	the middle leaves of the tobacco plant
Seoane	5in. long cigar with a ring gauge of 36
Sevillas	cigars made in Seville
Slim gauge	has a ring gauge between 26 and 38
Standard	4¾in. long cigar with a ring gauge of 40
Standard gauge	has a ring gauge between 39 and 44
tercios	bale of cured tobacco leaves
torcedore(s)	a tobacco roller
torpedo	specialized cigar shape, with pointed tip and non-parallel sides
Veguerito	5in. long cigar with a ring gauge of 37

Introduction

A Brief History of the Cigar

If you had to name one person who we should thank for introducing the western world to cigars, then without a shadow of a doubt that person would have to be Christopher Columbus. Though his discovery of natives smoking a certain leaf pales into insignificance in comparison with his discovery of the New World, it was nonetheless a momentous occasion on that day in 1492 when he first saw the blue smoke rising from the tubular bunches of leaves being inhaled by the local peoples.

Today, despite recent attitude changes, tobacco in various forms is smoked all over the world. People of every race, creed, and color smoke tobacco in some form. From the Inuits of Northern America to the tribes of the African continent, every nation has its smokers.

Smoking was not, however, an instant success with all sections of society. To begin with, it was very costly to import tobacco in quantity and it thus became the province of the rich—smoking was seen as a sign of wealth and good breeding. The habit spread from Spain throughout the rest of Europe, and as more trade routes were established between the New and Old Worlds, so the price of tobacco dropped and smoking became accessible to the majority of Europe's people.

In England smoking began in fits and starts. Tobacco was introduced in the reign of Elizabeth I by Sir Francis Drake. During this time tobacco—which was then smoked with the aid of a pipe—became immensely popular until the reign of James I. His now famous "Counterblast to Tobacco" put an end to the smoking pleasures of the English population. This, however, was to prove a minor glitch in the progression of the smoker. It was not so many years later that it occurred to those in power to put a tax on tobacco, thus giving smoking royal approval and earning the nation money to boot. It was not just in England that smoking was outlawed—it happened in Japan, the Middle East, and in Russia. Again, the power of tobacco overcame all the obstacles and grew ever stronger in popularity, earning vast fortunes for the plantation owners, merchants, and (not forgetting) the governments of the time.

Using tobacco in the form of cigars was not really appreciated in Britain until after the Peninsular War against Napoleon in the early part of the nineteenth century.

Above: Whatever would Raleigh have said? From its New World beginnings, tobacco conquered the world and to this day, the best product comes from across the Atlantic.

Until that time tobacco had been smoked through long clay pipes or inhaled as snuff. It was only when the troops returned home from Portugal and the Iberian Peninsula that cigars in their present form became popular. It was for this very reason that cigar factories were first opened in Britain with an 1821 Act of Parliament. Because of the tobacco duties levied on imported leaf, local cigar companies flourished and grew. However, people began to see a large difference in quality—those cigars being made in Britain were inferior, due to lack of experience in the manufacturing processes— imported cigars, and particularly those from Cuba, became increasingly popular and were seen as status symbols.

It was the Spanish, though, who became the big cigar smokers in Europe. This was because of their close links with Central and South America, much of which was at that time controlled by Spain, and Cuba was the ideal place for growing cigar tobacco. It had the climate, the soil type, and the tradition for rolling the finest quality cigars. King Ferdinand VII of Spain decreed in 1821 that cigar production in Cuba should be expanded to its maximum, and take over production of those cigars manufactured in Spain (known as Sevillas) and also cigars rolled in Britain. Meanwhile, in France and Britain, cigar smoking had really caught on; smoking rooms were established for gentlemen who wished to partake and the after dinner cigar became ever more popular. Queen Victoria had a brief stab at smoking, but her son Edward, Prince of Wales, later Edward VII, was a great fan of the cigar and it was with his famous words "Gentlemen, you may smoke," that cigar smoking found favor throughout the British Isles. Incidentally, a cigar bearing

Right: Originally designed to keep oily stains from gloves, today cigar bands are a colorful advertisement of the company of manufacture.

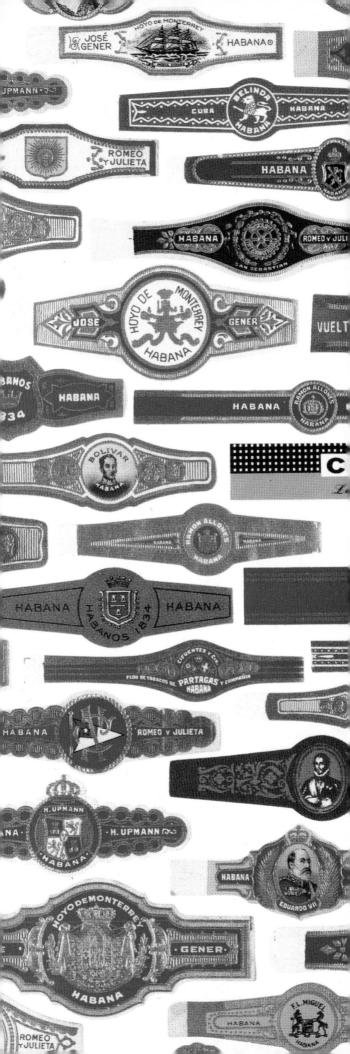

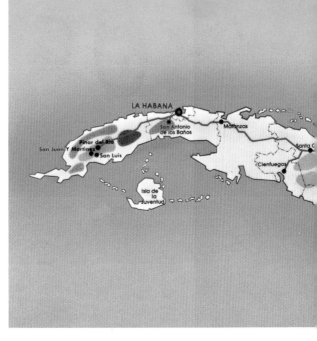

Edward's name is now one of the most popular cigars world-wide.

During Queen Victoria's reign Cuba was going through a turbulent phase, culminating in independence from Spain. At this time, many of the cigar-rolling families decided to leave Cuba because of the unrest. They moved to neighboring Caribbean islands such as Jamaica and Hispaniola (now the Dominican Republic and Haiti), setting up cigar factories in their new homes. Today many cigars are made on these islands—in fact, the Dominican Republic now produces many more cigars than Cuba, which although it has the reputation for making the finest cigars in the world, lost out on its major market, as we shall see.

Several important figures in the last century have been devotees of cigars; some have even given their names to certain sizes. The most obvious of these is Sir Winston Churchill, probably the most famous of all cigar-smoking statesmen. He was honored by having a very large cigar named after him—the Churchill. This size of cigar is now one of the most popular, a favorite of both young and old cigar smokers. To give you an idea of just how much Sir Winston enjoyed cigars; he is reputed to have smoked approximately 300,000 of them in his long and eventful life! Another who lent his name to a cigar

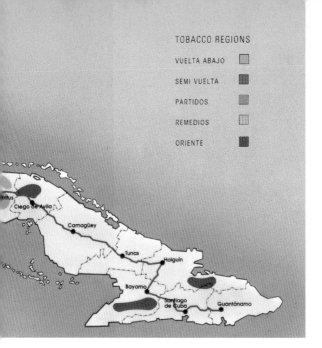

TOBACCO REGIONS

VUELTA ABAJO

SEMI VUELTA

PARTIDOS

REMEDIOS

ORIENTE

Above: The best tobacco producing area of the world? Probably! The west of Cuba boasts the Vuelta Abajo and Partidos regions, from where tobacco for many of the world's leading cigars is grown.

is Lord Lonsdale of boxing fame. The Lonsdale cigar is a particular favorite of mine, it is 6½in long and a shade over ¾in in diameter.

An American statesman who had a dramatic effect on cigar smoking was John F. Kennedy. He was a great devotee of the Havana cigar but in 1961, after the Bay of Pigs fiasco, he signed a declaration banning all trade between Cuba and the United States. He did, however, manage to secure a supply of his favorite smokes, the Petit Upmann, before outlawing Cuban cigars. In the morning before he was due to sign the declaration, he sent out his private secretary to purchase as many of his chosen cigars as possible. No sooner had the private secretary returned with 1,200 handmade smokes, the declaration was signed.

This trade embargo had a monumental effect on cigar sales and production. The cigar industry in Cuba, assisted—as was the whole of Cuba's economy—by Russian aid, prospered until the fall of Eastern European communism. Cuba went through a difficult phase during the early 1990s, not only due to lack of money for fertilizers and such, but also because of some very unseasonal weather. The com-

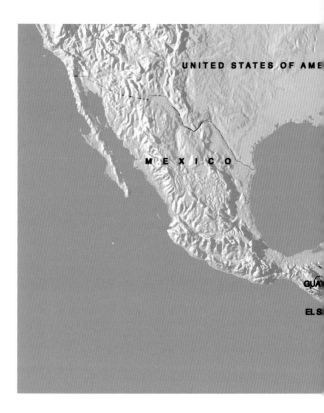

UNITED STATES OF AME

M E X I C O

GUA

EL S

bination of these factors meant that by 1994, cigar production fell to just under 50 million cigars. It is only recently, after investment in the cigar trade by other European countries, that production has started to increase.

Elsewhere, however, cigar producers rushed to fill the void created by Cuba's absence in the North American market-place. Brazil, the Dominican Republic, Honduras, Jamaica, Mexico, Nicaragua, and the United States itself were already cigar producers; but the embargo increased their importance substantially. Although each of these producers has had its trials and tribulations, none more so than Honduras and Nicaragua which were wracked by internal strife in the 1970s and 1980s, as we have seen, the Dominican Republic now produces more cigars than Cuba and Cuban emigres in the United States have helped that country's cigar industry, first as workers on imported Cuban tobacco and subsequently on blended non-Cuban tobaccos, including Connecticut shade, the only cigar tobacco grown in the US.

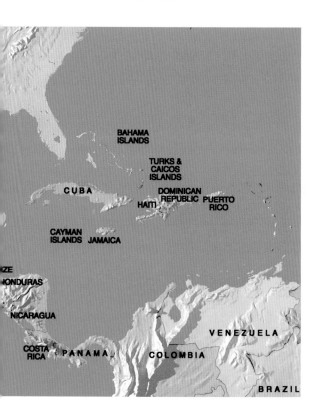

*Above: A map showing the Caribbean's major tobacco-
producing countries.*

This book looks at a selection of all
these cigars, concentrating on the best-
known premium cigars—in other words
truly hand-made cigars, rather than those
which are made by machine. What is the
difference? To understand that, we must
examine how cigars are made.

Machine-made Cigars
A cigar is basically a bundle of tobacco
rolled into a tubular shape, which is lit
at one end and smoked through the other.
Cigars are made up of three main parts:
the filler, the binder, and the wrapper.

• The filler is the part of the cigar which
gives the flavor. In machine-made cigars
the filler is usually made up of chopped
and shredded tobacco, rather like that
found in cigarettes. It sometimes consists
of low grade tobacco including the woody
stalks and stems from the plant.
• The next layer or binder is used to hold
the filler together. Better quality machined

cigars use a tobacco leaf for this. Lower quality and cheaper cigars use a material called H.T.L.—Homogenized Tobacco Leaf. H.T.L. is basically a sheet of paper which is made from scrap tobacco; the scraps are ground up, mixed with chemicals (to help combustion) and water then stretched and rolled into a large paper sheet.

• The last part of the cigar is its outer skin —the wrapper, which gives the cigar its smooth silky appearance.

Compared to hand-made cigars, machine-made cigars are inexpensive and easy to come by. They can be found and purchased anywhere that you can find cigarettes—newsagents, supermarkets, and gas stations. They need no special care to maintain their freshness and flavor, aside from a cellophane wrapper.

Hand-made Cigars
Hand-made cigars have had a starring role in the rebirth of cigar smoking. The largest increases in consumption have all involved hand-made cigars. They are made from the same components as machine-made cigars with the exception of one additional part which will be discussed below.

• The filler is the part of the cigar which gives the flavor. It is made up of a blend of three different types of leaf. These leaves—according to where they are taken from the plant—have different strengths, and it is a mixture of these three leaves which gives each particular cigar its distinctive flavor.
• The binder in hand-made cigars is always a part of a whole leaf. H.T.L. is never used in hand-made cigars. The sole purpose of the binder is to ensure that the filler is held in place correctly. It gives little or no flavor or strength to the cigar. It is a fairly rough-looking leaf and in some Cuban cigars two are used.

• The final element of the cigar is known as the wrapper. This is the part of the cigar which is most visible, and for this reason needs to be of the highest possible quality. The leaves are fairly vein-free and very thin and delicate.

Now, according to whether you are Cuban or Dominican, the wrapper leaf may or may not have any effect on the flavor of the cigar The Dominicans maintain that the wrapper can give up to 50 percent of the overall flavor of the cigar. The Cubans, on the other hand, maintain that the wrapper gives little to the flavor, but that it gives what is known as a "top-note" —the first taste you get when taking a puff on the cigar. What is not argued over, is that the wrapper leaf enhances the beauty and appearance of a well-made cigar.

Hand-rolled cigars are made roughly the same way in each country of manufacture, the main difference being the type of tobacco plant. In Cuba there are two, the Criollo and Corojo; others include those from Connecticut which produce some of the most flavorsome wrapper

Below: A selection of fine smokes available in the United States.

leaves in the world. As mentioned previously, there are three types of filler leaf grown. They are known as *ligero, seco* and *volado*. It is a blend of these three leaves which gives the cigar much of its characteristic tastes.

The *ligero* leaf is taken from the very top of the plant where growth is at its most vigorous, for this reason *ligero* is the strongest flavored of the filler leaves.

The second type of leaf, the *seco*, is larger in size than the *ligero* as it is slightly older and comes from lower down on the plant. This leaf is less highly flavored than the *ligero*.

Lastly, the *volado* is taken from the very bottom of the plant. This leaf gives very little to the taste and strength of the cigar, however it is used to balance the flavors of the *ligero* and *seco* leaves.

Few plants are capable of producing leaf of a fine enough quality to be used as wrapper—in Cuba wrapper comes from the *Corojo* plants, often grown under vast sheets of muslin cloth. This keeps the plant out of direct sunlight to ensure a pale-colored, ultra-fine quality leaf. Wrapper leaf grown in direct sunlight tends to be a little coarser and quite dark in color. Once it gets to the factory, wrapper leaf is graded into shades of brown (see page 24).

Young tobacco plants are planted in succession from October onwards, and take between 40 and 45 days to reach full maturity. A fully grown tobacco plant will reach upwards of 6ft. tall, with the leaves growing as large as 2ft. 6in. from tip to stem. As the tobacco plant matures, all flower buds and side shoots are stripped away to ensure that all growth is concentrated into producing large, healthy leaves.

The harvesting of the leaf begins in early January and continues through until late March. Harvesting the tobacco is the most labor-intensive part of the growing process, as each leaf must be individually picked by hand. No more than two or three leaves are picked from the plant at one time, with the remaining ones being taken from the stem, as and when, they become mature.

After harvesting, all the leaves are transported to large curing barns known as *Casas del Tabaco*. These are large, high, airy buildings where the tobacco is cured or tried. The leaves are tied into pairs and strung on to long poles. The poles are then hoisted high into the barn until the building is completely filled with tobacco. All the tobacco used for premium cigars is air-cured, meaning that it is left to cure naturally without being force-dried. This allows more of the flavor-giving oils to remain in the leaf.

It takes approximately 50 days for the leaves to become ready for the next stage of processing. During these 50 days the leaf turns from the natural green color to first yellow, and then to a rich golden brown.

When the curing process has been completed, the leaf must then be fermented. This is normally done twice, with a short break between curings, to sort the wrapper from the filler and binder After these processes are over—which together can take almost 90 days—the piles of fermenting leaves, known as *burros*, are taken apart and the leaves laid on airing racks to rest for a few days.

The cured tobacco leaves are then packed into large bales which are then wrapped in palm bark and sent to a holding warehouse. The leaf contained in the bales continues to develop and mature for several years.

Rolling the Cigar

Once the tobacco has matured in its tercios, it is sent to the factory to be turned into cigars. At the factory the tobacco is unpacked and prepared for use. The wrapper leaf must be moistened to make it flexible and to prevent it from becoming brittle and breaking. The large vein which runs down the center of the leaf is stripped out and discarded; each leaf is classified according to size, color, and texture. It is this stage which has led to one of the cigar world's longest and greatest myths. It is often wistfully said that cigars are rolled on a maiden's thigh—sadly this is not true; however, the stripping and sorting tasks are usually performed by women and it is thought that this is where the myth originates.

The filler and binder leaf need little other preparation except for removal of the central vein. These leaves have been matured for a considerable time—ranging from those which need to be aged for two years before they are ready to be turned into a cigar and those that mature quicker—sometimes in as little as 12 months.

Once the tobacco is unpacked and sorted, it is up to the blender to select the appropriate leaves for the correct blend for a particular type of cigar. Security around the blending room is kept high, as it is here that the secret recipes for each of the cigars is kept. When visiting a cigar factory it is quite an honor to be invited to see inside this area.

After the blender has gathered the particular ingredients, they are distributed amongst the rollers, who are seated at long wooden desks where they turn the leaves into cigars.

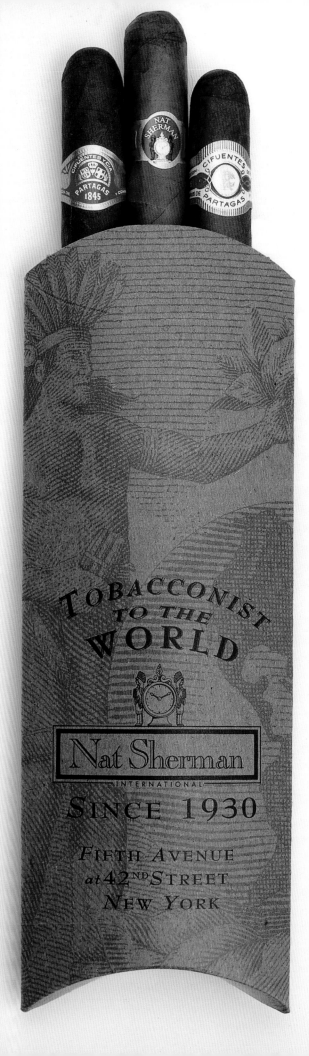

Whilst rolling the cigars, traditionally Cuban *torcedores* are read to. Classic works by authors such as Alexander Dumas and Shakespeare are read out, as well as Cuban and Spanish newspapers—not always the case elsewhere.

Now at last, the tobacco is ready to be rolled. The three types of filler are con-certinaed into a barrel shape which is then rolled into a binder leaf to form what is known as the bunch. Then it is placed into a mold to help it keep its uniform shape. Each of the different leaves is laid in a par-ticular direction. All the ends of the leaf that were nearest to the stem of the plant are laid pointing in the same direction: this is done because the tips of the leaf will taste lighter than the stem ends. This ensures that the finished cigar will have a gradual increase in strength when it is smoked.

The semi-finished cigars, or bunches as they are known, are kept in their molds for 24 hours during which time they have been placed in presses. This pressing ensures that the bunches retain their shapes without the need for gluing. Next, the wrapper leaf is rolled onto the bunch. This is done very carefully as it is very easy to damage the thin and fragile leaf. The wrapper is put on in a particular way which causes it to be self-binding—ensur-ing that the cigar does not unravel when smoked.

Lastly, a fourth and very important part is added to the cigar. This piece is known as the cap, and it is the only part of the cigar that is attached with glue. It is used to cover one end of the cigar and is glued with a tasteless and odorless vegetable gum made from the tragacanth plant. On some cigars, a different method of sealing the end is used. This involves twisting a piece of the actual wrapper, resembling a small pigtail, around the head of the cigar. This method is only ever used on hand-made cigars, usually of the best quality, and never appears on machine-made cig-

Above: Nat Sherman opened his first tobacco shop in New York City in 1930. Today the family company makes and sells cigars and smoking products around the world.

ars. During all these processes the only tool used other than the roller's hands is a flat blade known as a *chaveta*. The *chaveta* is used to trim the leaf to the right size and shape, and is also used to help roll the cigar into its final smoothly parallel shape. The cigar is then placed in a guillotine and is trimmed to the exact size. It is also put through a gauge, known as a ring gauge, to check that it is of an even diameter all along its length.

In Cuba there are four grades of rollers, numbered from four to seven, grade four being the lowest and grade seven the highest and most skilful. It takes at least a year to train a *torcedor* to grade one competence and up to 20 years for a roller to attain grade seven.

Junior rollers are given the task of making small, narrow gauge cigars and they also help in some of the tobacco processing stages. It is only the top grade rollers that are capable of rolling the more complicated sizes such as the torpedo and *figurado*—cigars with pointed tips and sides that are not parallel. The *torcedores* are paid directly in relation to their grading. Consequently, large cigars cost more to purchase not only because they use more tobacco than smaller sizes, but also because the roller is being paid more than his less skilful colleagues.

Once the cigars have been rolled they are tied together into bundles of 50 called *medias ruedas*. A small piece of paper listing information such as the roller's name and the brand and size of the cigars is placed into the bundle, which is then taken to the quality control department. Here, several cigars are taken out of the bundle. Each is measured to ensure that its length and diameter is consistent with standard. Also, and most importantly, the cigars are weighed to ensure they are within set parameters. This is crucial to ensure the cigars have a uniform draw when being smoked. If the cigar weighs too much, then too much tobacco has been rolled into it. This will cause the draw to be too tight, giving a difficult and very unsatisfactory smoke. Conversely, if the cigar weighs too little, then the draw will been too easy, causing the cigar to burn quickly and at too hot a temperature. This has the effect of making the cigar a bitter and acrid smoke.

Only after passing these checks are the cigars moved on to the next stage. Whilst the cigars are being rolled, the tobacco is kept quite moist to facilitate ease of rolling. This moisture must now be removed. The bundles of 50 cigars are placed into large cedar cupboards in a room called the *escaparate* or conditioning room. The cigars are kept in this room for up to three weeks for a Cuban cigar and, in some more expensive Dominican cigars, up to 18 months.

During this period of time, moisture levels in the cigars are dramatically reduced. Another and very important process occurs in this room, and that is the blending and marrying of the flavors and aromas in the different parts of the cigar. Only after going through these phases can the cigar be smoked to its full enjoyment and with further aging can be improved even more.

Next, the cigars are passed to the color-grading room, which is known as the *escogida*. Color-grading cigars is a highly skilled job—there are more than 65 differ-

Above: A box of Montechristos showing evenness of color range, shape, banding, and manufacture.

ent hues in which cigars are available. A color grader can earn almost as much as a top roller. These 65 shades of color are divided into four main groups.

- *Claro*. These cigars are a pale golden-yellow color.
- *Colorado claro*, a mid-brown color, slightly darker than *claro*.
- *Colorado*, a darker reddish-brown color.
- *Maduro*, which is a dark, plain chocolate *color*.

There are two other colors which you may come across, although probably not with Cuban cigars. They are *candela* and *oscuro*. *Candela*-colored cigars have a pale green wrapper, and were once very popular in America though now far less so. The other color, *oscuro*, is almost black. *Oscuro* wrapper leaves are grown in direct sunlight and are often dipped in boiling water to make them very dark. Cigars this dark were popular at the turn of the century; they are not often produced today.

After the cigars have been color-graded, they are placed into their boxes by the graders. Then the boxes are passed to the banding department to have their characteristic cigar bands attached. The banders are usually women because their hands are more dextrous. They must remove only one cigar at a time from the box and replace it in exactly the same position from which it was taken to ensure that the order of cigars chosen by the color grader is maintained. A full box of cigars will be the same color overall, but there may be a slight graduation from darker on the left through to a slightly lighter color on the right of the box.

The cigar bands themselves are attached with a tiny pin-prick of the same vegetable glue used for sealing the cap of the cigar. Interestingly, cigars were originally produced without bands. That is until gentlemen, who in the last century wore white gloves when smoking, noticed that their gloves were becoming stained with unsightly tars from the cigars. A request was made that a plain paper band should be wrapped around the cigar to avoid this problem. A Dutchman, named Gustav Bock, has been credited with introducing highly decorated, branded bands onto cigars—why not advertise your cigars as they are being smoked?

Cigar Packaging

Hand-made or premium cigars are available in a range of packaging—everything from a single tube to a box of 50 and sometimes even boxes of 100.

The type of box most often seen is known simply as the flat-dressed box. This is a flatish cedar box which contains 25 cigars in two layers: one of 13 cigars (the top layer) and one of 12 cigars plus a wooden or cardboard "blank" to stop the bottom layer from shifting during transit. The two layers are separated by a thin sheet of cedar to help maintain freshness. The box is dressed with the colorful, eye-catching designs of each particular brand.

Quite often it will be noticed that the cigars from this type of box are square, or very nearly so, in cross-section. This is because the boxes are often pressed—so

Above: A Nat Sherman Hampton.

squashing slightly the cigars inside. Most of the major manufacturers produce cigars in this type of box and they are certainly the most common to be seen stacked on cigar merchants' shelves.

The next most commonly produced type of packaging is the slide-lid box or cabinet. This is a plain cedar box which contains a bundle of 25 or 50 cigars tied with a yellow silk ribbon. The box will have the manufacturer's name branded into the lid and sides, but otherwise has little or no decoration. The cigars contained in cabinet selection boxes are just as they appear from the roller's bench—in other words, unpressed—and are the favorites of many a cigar connoisseur.

Another method of presenting cigars is in a box know as the S.B.N., or *semi-boîte nature*. This type is a cross between the cabinet and the flat box. It is made, as always, from natural cedar, but unlike the flat box it is rather plain, having no decoration save for the name of the cigar branded into the lid. Again, as in the cabinet box, the cigars in an S.B.N. are unpressed.

The last type of box is one that is fairly uncommon and is known simply as the 8-9-8 box. It is called this because instead of having two layers of 12 and 13 cigars, it has three layers of eight, nine and again eight cigars, thus making up a box of 25.

More often than not, these boxes are varnished and are reserved for very high quality cigars. Like the cabinet and S.B.N. boxes, the cigars remain unpressed.

Mention must also be given to cigars in aluminum tubes. Most brands produce at least two or three sizes packed this way. It is a very convenient way of buying single cigars, but most aficianados tend to steer clear. They are ideal if traveling because of the protection afforded to the cigar. Unfortunately, they are rarely airtight and the cigar will begin to dry out after a couple of weeks if not smoked.

Cigar Sizes

Hand-made cigars are available in a bewildering array of sizes from the very small to the very large and in a variety of different thicknesses. To make matters even more confusing, different manufacturers use the same names for different shapes, or different names for similar shapes!

Above (from left to right): Cigar sizes—Montecristo "A," a 9¼in. long Gran corona; Nat Sherman Dakota, 7in. long; Honduran-made Don Ramos No. 19 Epicure, 4½in. long.

Cigars are usually grouped into three basic divisions—heavy gauge, standard gauge and slim gauge. The gauge or diameter of the cigars is measured in a rather antiquated term called "ring gauge." This is measured in ⅟₆₄s of an inch. Therefore, a cigar with a ring gauge of 64 will be one inch in diameter and a cigar with a 32 ring gauge will have a diameter of half an inch.

A heavy gauge cigar has a ring gauge between 45 and 52. Standard gauge would be between 39 and 44, and a slim gauge cigar anywhere between 26 and 38. The length of a cigar is measured in inches in the United Kingdom and America, but in millimetres in Europe. Listed below is a guide to the main sizes of the most popular cigars.

Cigar Name	Length	Diameter
Heavy gauge		
Gran corona	9¼	47
Double corona	7⅝	49
Churchill	7	47
Corona extra	5⅝	46
Robusto	4⅞	50
Piramide	6⅛	52
Standard gauge		
Lonsdale	6½	42
Corona	5½	42
Petit corona	5	42
Tres petit corona	4⅜	42
Slim gauge		
Especiale	7½	38
Especiale No. 2	6	38
Panatela	see below	

Amongst these cigars are a couple of shapes and sizes which are slightly out of the ordinary. The first of these is the heavy gauge *piramide*—this is a cigar whose end tapers to a closed point and is often mistakenly called a torpedo. At present, these cigars can be rather hard to find, as they are made only in very small quantities by the most skilled of the cigar rollers.

Another unusual type is known as the *panetela*. The term "panatela" is unfortunately rather loose as this type of cigar can be of various lengths and diameters. However, suffice it to say, that a panatela is generally a very slim cigar which can either be short or long!

One more type of cigar which you may see is the *figurado*—the true torpedo-shaped cigar. These have a point at both ends and were the favored shape for stylish smokers at the turn of the century. Again, like panatela, figurado is a loose term, though this type of cigar is usually of a standard to medium gauge and can be of several different lengths

Generally speaking, the thicker the diameter or ring gauge of a cigar, the more complex the flavors will be. This is due to the fact that there is physically more tobacco than in a slimmer cigar and, also, that a thick cigar will burn more slowly, giving a cooler and smoother smoke. Small thin cigars tend to burn at a quicker rate because air is drawn through at a greater velocity thus sometimes producing a hot and acrid smoke.

Storage of Hand-Made Cigars

As with all natural products, careful storage is necessary to maintain the peak condition of cigars. Cigars which have not been looked after properly will very rapidly deteriorate and lose their flavor and become totally unsmokable.

By far the most crucial aspect of caring for cigars is to keep them at the correct humidity. Unless they are stored in a fairly damp environment, cigars will dry out and the precious, flavor-giving oils will evaporate leaving a nasty bitter, acrid smoke. The ideal humidity for keeping cigars any length of time is between 70 and 72 percent relative humidity. The average level of humidity in the home is approximately 45 to 50 percent—even less for air-conditioned buildings, so just how does one maintain 72 percent humidity?

There are two ways around this problem. The first, if you smoke only a few cigars a week, is to pay regular visits to your local cigar merchant and buy cigars only as and when you want to smoke them. He will have, at the very least, a large humidified cabinet in which to store cigars, thus ensuring everything you will buy is stored correctly. This will also have the added advantage of building a relationship between you and the merchant. He will then be able to advise you more accurately as to the type of cigar which is right for you and, also, if any hard-to-find cigars come into stock, you will have a head start over other, less regular customers. Several cigar stores will also keep larger stocks of your cigars in humidified conditions if they have the facilities.

The other, and possibly more convenient, way of storing cigars yourself (unless your neighbor is a cigar shop!) is to purchase a humidor. This is a small wooden box which will hold between 50 and 300 cigars. Attached to the inside of the lid is a device which will release humidity so keeping the interior of the box at exactly the correct level. Most humidors are lined with Spanish cedar, which is less resinous than other types. Occasionally, mahogany is used to line humidors—this has a similar effect to cedar—maintaining the taste without adding any strong flavors. The box itself will be available in a vast range of finishes, something to suit every possible taste. They also come in a large range of prices. When buying one, remember that the main objective is for the box to take care of your cigars, so it is definitely worth having a chat with your cigar dealer as to which companies make the most effective humidifier units. It is no good spending $2,500 on a beautiful looking box if it doesn't keep your cigars humid!

The humidifier unit itself is usually made of a durable plastic or metal. Contained inside the shell is a material which is able to absorb and release moisture at a set rate. Some brands contain fluid which must be used periodically to maintain the material inside. Distilled or de-ionised water should always be used to refill these units. If tap water is used, chemicals and calcium deposits will build up making the unit less effective and can even stop it working altogether.

When deciding which humidor to purchase, there are several important considerations to remember. The most important of these is the size: many people buy too small a humidor to begin with, then six months later when they decide that they really enjoy smoking cigars, have to purchase another! Try to buy a humidor larger than you think you will actually need, then you will not need to buy another.

Another important thing to keep in mind is how long a humidifier can go between refills. The last thing you want to happen is to return from a holiday or busi-

Above: Cigars are certainly protected in tubes but to maintain the correct humidity a humidor is preferable. This is a box of Cuesta-Rey Aristocrats in their glass tubes.

ness trip to find your supply of expensive hand-made cigars has dried out! Make sure that a period of at least a month goes by before the unit needs refilling—if not, choose a different humidor.

Often a humidor will have a small dial or hygrometer inside. This is intended to indicate the humidity level inside the box. Be warned! Most of these are very inaccurate, and can be as much as 15 percent out of true. It is much better to purchase a humidor with a system that can self-regulate the humidity to 70 percent. As with any cigar-related questions, talk to your merchant.

Temperature is also reasonably important and should be maintained at approximately 70°F (21°C). If the temperature is too low, you will always have problems keeping the humidity high enough. This is due to the scientific fact that cold air cannot physically hold a high level of moisture. A worrying time for storing cigars is in winter, when there is snow on the ground—ambient humidity will then be around the zero level.

Conversely, too high a temperature will see humidity levels rise too much. High temperature in conjunction with high humidity leads to mold. This should not be confused with cigar bloom or plume.

Mold is greenish-blue in color and gives off a musty smell. Cigar bloom is a good sign. It is a reaction between moist air and the aromatic oils in the cigar. It is white in color and is odorless. If you spot mold on your cigars, remove them and dispose of them. Then open the lid of the humidor until the humidity returns to normal.

If you cannot afford or do not smoke enough to warrant the purchase of a humidor, all is not entirely lost. Ask your cigar dealer for some sealable polythene bags. These are ideal for keeping cigars in reasonable condition for a couple of months Do not, however, store cigars in a refrigerator as some people recommend. The temperature is far too low to enable a suitable humidity level to build up and your cigars will very rapidly dry out and become unsmokable.

If by some misfortune, your cigars do become dried out, do not throw them away immediately. If they have been dry for only a couple of weeks it is possible for them to be reconditioned. This must be done slowly, over a period of several weeks. If you try to put them straight into a humidor with a 70 percent humidity they will split and be useless. This is because the filler tobacco will expand at a quicker rate than the wrapper. Start with a low humidity, say 50 percent, and then gradually build it up over a period of three or four weeks. Hopefully, your cigars will then once again be able to be smoked.

Aging and Maturing Cigars
Many new smokers ask the question, "How long does a cigar keep for?" Rather like fine wine, cigars will keep, so long as they are stored in the correct climate, for many years. Not only do they keep for a long time, but they actually get better as they mature. As the aromatic oils age, they become more mature and mellow, giving the smoke a delicious smoothness with not a hint of bitterness. Hand-made cigars will, in general, improve for up to 15 years

Above: Cabinet boxes are excellent vehicles for maturation of cigars because within them the cigars are not separated from contact with each other.

and some, particularly very oily cigars, will last much longer.

Some years ago, all cigars imported from Cuba would be aged for a couple of years before they were released for sale. Sadly, this is no longer possible as the demand is so high and the production too small.

When cigars are to be aged, the humidity level needs to be somewhat lower than that needed when they are to be smoked. A level of humidity between 58 and 63 percent is recommended. This not only assists the maturation process but also cuts down any risk that mold may develop. Cigars loose in a small, home-size humidor will not mature properly either, as after some time, the varying flavors of different cigars will blend together and they will eventually all taste the same. Ideally, cigars which are going to be aged need to be kept in their original boxes, so a small humidor is not ideal. A large, cupboard-sized humidor will be needed to age any decent quantity of cigars. Some of the larger cigar stores will have specialized facilities for this purpose, the better ones being able to supply personal large, cedar-lined lockers where upwards of 20 or 30 boxes can be stored.

Any box of cigars can be matured but some are better than others, and will continue to improve for a lot longer, particularly dark and oily cigars. The more oil a cigar has, the longer it will maintain its flavors, although all cigars, no matter how oily, will begin to lose their flavor after approximately 15 years. Next, it helps dramatically if you can find cabinet boxes of 25 cigars. Better still, cabinets of 50 will be even better when aged. Flat boxes and S.B.N. cigars will age but they are separated from each other by a cedar sheet. In a cabinet box, all the cigars remain in contact with each other and a better, more even, maturation will occur.

Recently, with the cigar boom at its height, pre-embargo and pre-Castro cigars have become much sought after. These cigars were made more than 35 years ago and command exceedingly high prices—upwards of $4,000 for a box of 25! A word of warning, however, for those thinking about purchasing a box of cigars as old as this; there can be, sometimes, no guarantee of how these cigars have been stored. Although when purchased, usually at auction, they appear to be in good condition, there may have been a very long time when they have been left to completely dry out. If you do want to invest in old cigars make sure they have a documented history, and ideally have been looked after for their entire life by a reputable cigar dealer.

Counterfeit Cigars
Unfortunately, due to the huge demand for Cuban cigars, and the lack of supply, counterfeit cigars are becoming ever more frequent. These cigars look very similar to the real thing, even down to the bands. Remember, there's a lot of money to be made here, so counterfeiters have become very adept at rolling good-looking cigars and acquiring the authentic looking boxes and bands to place them in. These cigars are highly likely to be made in somebody's front room in downtown Havana, or, nowhere near Cuba at all. Often, fake cigars will contain not just low grade

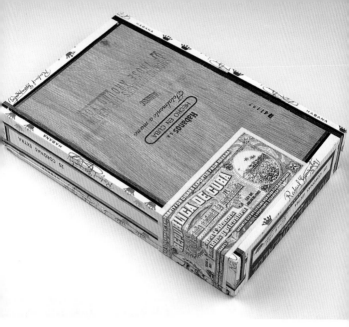

Above: The information given on a box of Cuban cigars helps to identify fake or counterfeit cigars. Each box of Havanas has on its top the chevron Habanos *(Havanas). On its base (here seen on a box of 25 Rafael Gonzalez Coronas Extra) are the three "hallmarks"—the name of the Cuban company exporting Havanas (Habanbos S.A.),* Hecho en Cuba *(Made in Cuba), and* Totalmente a mano *(totally by hand). Binding the box is the Cuban Government Warranty Seal.*

tobacco, but other plant material or even newspaper. Even if they look and smell right, the blend inside will be non-existent and taste revolting.

All real Havanas have a number of distinguishing features on the box to prove they are the genuine article. First, look out for the green, Cuban Government Warranty seal on the lid and front edge of the box. Turn the box over and branded into the base you will see several things: the words *"Hecho en Cuba,"*—made in Cuba—and *"Totalemente a Mano"*—completely by hand, will appear below the words "Habanos S.A." A ground of letters, the date and factory stamps will be rubber-stamped on the bottom of the box. In 1994 a stick-on "Habanos S.A." chevron also appeared on one corner of the top of the box. Real Cuban cigars must have all these features; if they do not, then do not buy. If in any doubt at all ask your cigar dealer to verify them. It is a wise precaution not to buy any Cuban cigars offered cheaply, especially by tourists returning from Cuba who think they can make a fast buck—they will

almost without exception be counterfeit. You have been warned!

Choosing your Cigars

As with every other commodity, everybody has their own favorite brand, size, and shape of cigar. Some prefer large full-bodied cigars with dark wrapper leaves; some prefer the opposite. For beginners, the best advice is to try as many different types of cigar in as many different sizes until you find one that suits your particu-

Above: The splendid walk-in humidor at Havana Club on Sloane Street.

lar taste. But how can you tell whether a cigar is in good shape or not?

The first thing to do when selecting cigars is to make absolutely sure that the shop from which you are buying has the cigar stored in a humidified cabinet, at the very least, or better still in a walk-in humidor. Some shops will keep their cigars in better condition than others. It is not normally a good idea to buy tubed cigars from a local corner newsagent—they will have a very slow turnover and the cigars may have been lying around for several years without being humidified. When buying hand-made cigars, it is really necessary to go to a specialist.

Once you have chosen your cigar shop and seen the humidor, the next thing is to find the right size of cigar. The first thing to do is to pick up them and feel them. Which feels most comfortable? This done, inspect the cigars closely. The wrappers of all the cigars in one box ought to be the same color. The leaf itself should be smooth and without many veins—it should also have a silky, shiny quality to it. Be fairly careful when handling cigars in the shop—don't forget that a cigar you pick up to look at and then decide not to buy will be purchased by someone else—the quickest way to find yourself out of favor with a cigar merchant is to harm his cigars!

When you want to check that the cigar has been kept in the proper conditions, NEVER pick it up and roll it by your ear. This is something that looks good in the movies but it will tell you absolutely nothing about the cigar. Worse still, it can damage the fragile outer wrapper leaf and compress the filler. This irritating habit is know as "listening to the band" and is practiced by people who pretend to know about cigars but in reality know nothing! All one needs to do to check the condition of a cigar is gently to squeeze it between forefinger and thumb. It should feel firm and springy. If it is too moist it will feel spongy—the excess moisture makes it difficult to keep the cigar alight, resulting in a very unsatisfying smoke. If the cigar is too dry, then it will pop and crack as you gently squeeze it: again, reject it and choose another. You must be very careful when you squeeze; do it too hard and you will damage the cigar. On top of this, try to make sure you do not squeeze near to

Cigar cutters and piercers are made in many shapes and sizes.

the cap end, as you will run the risk of "popping" the cap off.

Many smokers like to smell the cigar, although this habit will not tell you a great deal about how it will smoke. What it can do, however, is tell you whether any foreign, odiferous substances—for example aftershave or furniture polish—have come into contact with the box. If this is so, not only will you there be a smell, but if you were to light the cigar you would be able to taste it!

Once you are happy with your choice of cigar it is at last time to smoke it.

Preparing a Cigar for Smoking

There is an art to preparing a cigar for smoking. If done properly, it can enhance one's enjoyment of a cigar and, for some, becomes almost a ritual.

The first thing that needs to be done is to open up the closed end of the cigar. There is a special tool made just for this purpose—the cigar cutter. There are several types of cutter on the market, the most popular being a single-bladed guillotine. This tool removes a complete section from the cap of the cigar giving a nice clean draw. When using this type of cutter, it is important not to cut too deep. Look at where the cap joins the cigar and you will see a distinct line all the way around the circumference. Do not cut below this line as this is the only part of the cigar that is anchored and is holding the entire cigar together. A cut of ⅛in. (2–3mm.) depth from the tip is sufficient. When cutting a *figurado* or *pyramide* most people prefer to remove about ⅓in. (7–8mm.), still ensuring that you don't go below the line of the cap.

Other smokers like to remove a part of the cap with a V-cutter, sometimes called a Cat's Eye cutter due to the shape of the cut it leaves. This is not by any means a bad method of cutting a cigar, but it has a couple of drawbacks. You do not get such a large cross-section of the cigar through

Above: Preparing the cigar—be careful about the depth of your cut. Ensure you do not cut too far from the tip or you will cause the cigar to lose its wrapper.

which the smoke can be drawn. This will speed up the burning time of the cigar, affording a slightly harsher smoke. Additionally, it is impossible to have the blades on this type of cutter sharpened once they have become dulled with use. Incidentally, you cannot cut a *pyramide* or *figurado* with a V-cutter.

Some accessory companies produce cigar piercers, a small, pointed, needle-like tool used to prod holes in the cap of the cigar. This is not recommended by any true cigar lover. As the piercer goes through the cap, it compresses the filler into a hard and compact lump just under the cap. As the smoke passes over this lump, it condenses out unpleasant tasting tars and oil. Also, it directs smoke straight onto the very tip of your tongue making for a harsh smoke.

Below: Lighting options—it is always preferable to use a long cedarwood match, but if want to use a lighter, for pity's sake don't use a petrol-filled one: you'll absolutely ruin the taste of the cigar.

The one thing cigar smokers will always be arguing about is whether or not to remove the cigar band. It makes no difference to how the cigar is smoked whether the band is on or off. In the United States it is generally accepted that the band should stay on, whereas in the United Kingdom and Europe it is often seen as bad form to be showing off your cigar brand. If you do wish to remove the band, don't do it before you light up. Often the band is stuck to the cigar and when you try to remove it you will remove the wrapper too. Wait until you have smoked about ½in. (1½cm.), the cigar by then will have warmed up enough to loosen the glue, so enabling the band to be removed without damaging the wrapper. It is a good idea for cigar novices to leave the band on, as it is a handy marker for how far down the cigar should be smoked.

The last part of the preparation is to light the cigar. This needs to be done carefully. First, you need to use an odorless

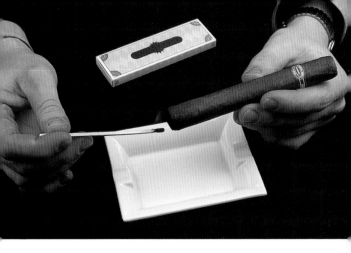

Above: Lighting a cigar—rotate the cigar over a neutral flame until it chars and starts to take. Blow on the end to ensure that it burns evenly. Take your time!

heat source such as a long cedar match or a butane lighter. Do not use a lighter which uses a liquid fuel—the odor from the flame will be drawn into the cigar and the flavor ruined. Place the end of the cigar horizontally into the flame and slowly rotate so that the entire tip is charred. At this stage the cigar is not yet in the mouth; now is the time to place the cigar in the mouth. Light a second match and, holding the cigar about ½in. (1½cm.) above the flame and draw through the cigar, slowly

rotating all the time. (This can prove tricky to begin with but you will soon learn with practice and be able to do it without thinking.) You will see the flame jump to the end of the cigar and, if rotated properly, you will have a perfectly lit cigar.

Smoke the cigar slowly—one or two puffs per minute is enough to give you a satisfying smoke without making the cigar burn too hot. A cigar is to be savored, not smoked in great gulps; it should be sipped as if you were drinking a vintage cognac. Do not inhale the smoke, the taste alone ought to be enough. Some smokers like to dip the unlit end of a cigar into a glass of port or cognac. This is a shame as it ruins the flavor of the smoke—would you mix vintage cognac with coke? Last of all make sure you have time to smoke; a good cigar should never be rushed as the enjoyment will be diminished.

Do not tap the ash from the end of a cigar, let it build naturally because it will keep the cigar burning at the correct temperature. Let it fall naturally, preferably into an ashtray—though there are some who maintain nothing does a carpet better than a good sprinkling of cigar ash!

When it is time to extinguish a cigar, do not stub it out, as this will have the effect of igniting the burnt oils—giving off an unpleasant odor. Simply lay it in an ashtray and it will quickly die, leaving no lingering smell.

The Cigars

Included in this section are a selection of the most popular premium cigars—Havanas, cigars from the Dominaican Republic and the United States: all fine smokes. In general, Cuban cigars are much richer in strength and have a more complex flavor than non-Cuban brands. Indeed those who have never smoked a cigar before would be best advised to begin with a milder smoking Dominican cigar so that they can accustomize themself with the type of flavor that cigars give and, importantly, to acquaint themself to the feel and size of a cigar. Only after getting used to smoking cigars should one attempt to try a full-flavored Havana such as a Bolivar.

I have not gone into great depth about flavors; each person will taste the same cigar differently—leave the hint of chocolate, the blast of blackcurrant, and the taste of leather to the wine buffs!

The lengths of the cigars are given first in inches and then by ring gauge

Above: A distinctive Cuban Partagas 8-9-8
(Varnished Box) filled with the 6¾in. 43 gauge cigars.

Arturo Fuente

The Fuente family has been producing very high quality cigars since the early 1900s but has only recently started growing its own tobacco on the Chateau de la Fuente plantation.

One of the ranges, the Fuente Fuente Opus X, usually uses tobacco from the Dominican Republic for every part including the wrapper. Most other Dominican cigars have wrappers from other countries, mainly Cameroon and the United States. Unfortunately, at the moment, the Opus X is in very limited supply and is not yet available in the United Kingdom, even in America most smokers are limited to buying two cigars only!

The Opus X is remarkably full-bodied, and is smoked with a smoothness to match.

Name	Length	Ring Gauge
Opus X Range		
Reserva "A"	9¼	47
Double Corona	7⅞	49
Reserva No. 1	6⅝	44
Reserva No. 2	61	52
Petit Lanceros	6¼	38
Fuente Fuente	5⅝	46
Robusto	5¼	50

Right: Two views of the Opus X band on a Robusto.

Bolivar

This full-flavored cigar was named after the nineteenth century revolutionary Simon Bolivar—probably the only man in history to have both a country and a cigar given his name. Bolivar is Cuba's fullest-flavored cigar and is definitely not recommended as a first cigar, although once accustomed to smoking, they make a great after dinner smoke.

Available in a range of sizes to suit all tastes, Bolivar cigars are relatively cheap compared with other brands. Favorite sizes include the heavyweight Belicosos Finos, a torpedo or pointed cigar, and the Royal Corona. The Corona Extra is probably the fullest-flavored of them all. A selection of the available sizes is listed below.

Name	Length	Ring Gauge
Corona Gigantes	7	47
Churchill (tubed)	7	47
Lonsdale	6½	42
Corona Extra	5⅝	44
Belicosos Finos	5½	52
Corona	5½	42
Petit Corona	5½	42
Royal Corona	4⅞	50
Corona Junior	4¼	42

*Left and Above: A box and single example of the Bolivar
Corona Gigantes, a fine, full-flavored smoke.*

Cohiba

The name Cohiba—one of the most important in cigar history—is believed to come from the Cuban Taino Indian word for cigar. Originally produced in Cuba only in small quantities solely for diplomatic use—nobody was able to buy a box commercially—in 1982 Cubatobacco decided that the time was right to launch the brand and allow Cohiba cigars onto the market. The story from then is, in microcosm, the story of the cigar manufacturing since the U.S. embargo of Cuban products.

The Montecristi factory in the Dominican Republic, famous for its cigars some of which mirror Cuban brands, began making its Cohibas in the 1980s, registering the trademark in 1992. Thus there were two Cohiba brands on the market—Cuban and Dominican—with the latter available in the United States through Global Direct Marketing. On top of this, the General Cigar Corporation also started to pro-duce Cohibas (known as "red spot" Cohibas because of the red in the "O") and registered the trademark Cohiba in 1992. The complex trademark issues that this engenders are likely to come to law for resolution.

The G.C.M. Cohibas come in nine sizes, from Churchill (7in. long, ring gauge 49) to Corona Minor (4in. long, 42 ring gauge). They are made from a Cameroon wrapper, Dominican filler, and Indonesian binder.

The Montecristi de Tabacos

Right: The G.C.M. Cohibas are distinguishable by the red infill in the letter "O" of Cohiba.

Dominican Cohibas are produced in a variety of lengths including the following:

Name	Length	Ring Gauge
Bocado	4	46
Esplendido	7	47
Jibarito	6½	44
Robusto	5	46
Lanceros	7½	39
Corona Especial 1	7	42
Corona Especial 2	6⅞	40

The Cuban Cohibas, on the other hand, are probably the most expensive cigars in the world being about 40 percent more expensive to buy than other Cuban brands.

There are two ranges within the brand, the first being known as the Linea Classica or "classic line." This range consists of six sizes including the superbly large and powerful Esplendido, the short and heavy gauge Robusto, and the slim elegant Panatela. Strength in this range depends on size of cigar, with the smallest being mild to medium in strength, and the larger sizes being full and powerful smokes.

The second range was launched in London amidst a blaze of publicity in November 1993. The range is known as the Linea 1492 and marks the 500th anniversary of the discovery of the New World, There are only five sizes in the range named Siglo (century) I-V. They are all of medium body and the preferred size is the Siglo IV.

Right and Overleaf: The Cohiba Lanceros is the longest of the Linea Classica at 7½in.; note the pigtail end, an alternative to the more usual cap.

Name	Length	Ring Gauge
Linea Classica		
Lanceros	7½	38
Esplendido	7	47
Corona Especial	6	38
Exquisito	5	36
Robusto	4⅞	50
Panatela	4½	26
Linea 1492		
Siglo V	6⅝	43
Siglo IV	5⅝	46
Siglo III	6⅛	42
Siglo II	5	42
Siglo I	4	40

Cuaba

This brand is the latest addition to the range of Cuban cigars and is rather special. Launched in the autumn of 1996 in London, they take their name from a flammable Cuban bush!

This is a small range of cigars, numbering only four, each being a figurado or double-tapered cigar. Initially, stocks were made in precisely the same way that cigars were made at the turn of the century. Molds were not used and the cigars were of slightly different diameters. These first cigars have now become collectors items.

Now made in the Romeo y Julieta factory in Havana, they are medium in strength and are an excellent smoke.

Name	Length	Ring Gauge
Exclusivos	5⅝	46
Generosos	5¼	42
Tradicionales	4¾	42
Divinos	4	43

Above and Right: The double-tapered Exclusivos—medium in strength and an excellent smoke.

Cuesta-Rey

The famous brand Cuesta-Rey recently celebrated its centenary. It is owned by the Newman family, one of the oldest established cigar-making families in the United States. To celebrate this unique occasion a book has been published, tracing the history of the cigar and the family who produced it.

Cuesta-Rey hand-made cigars are widely available in the United States and UK, coming in a complete range of sizes, with one of the largest—the Aristocrat—being packaged individually in glass tubes. They are all mild in flavor and are ideal during the daytime, perhaps after a light lunch. Some of the sizes are available in a choice of claro or maduro wrapper leaves.

Name	Length	Ring Gauge
No. 1	8½	52
No. 2	7¼	48
Aristocrat	7¼	48
Captiva (tubed)	6³⁄₁₆	42
No. 5	5½	43
Robusto	4½	50

Above and Right: A box of Cuesta-Rey's Aristocrats, 7¼in. 48 gauge cigars which are packaged in individual glass tubes.

Davidoff

Zino Davidoff, the founder of this brand, was a Russian émigré born in Kiev at the beginning of the century, who died in 1994 after a long and eventful life. He eventually made his home in Geneva where he created his own brand of cigars.

Originally produced in Cuba, Davidoff cigars are of the highest order; however, for various reasons he moved his company production to the Dominican Republic in March 1990. The Cuban cigars bearing his name were easily the equal of any Cuban brand, including Cohiba. Nowadays, Davidoff cigars are available in a range of three different strengths from mild, through medium, to full.

Name	Length	Ring Gauge
Light		
Anniversario No. 1	8⅔	48
Anniversario No. 2	7	48
No. 1	7½	38
No. 2	6	38
No. 3	5⅛	30
Ambassadrice	4⅝	26
Medium		
1000	4⅝	34
2000	5	42
3000	4	33
4000	6³⁄₃₂	42
5000	5⅝	46
Full		
Grand Cru 1	6³⁄₃₂	42
Grand Cru 2	5⅝	42
Grand Cru 3	5	42
Grand Cru 4	4⅝	40
Grand Cru 5	4	40

Right: A Davidoff 5000—a medium-strength cigar.

Don Ramos

These finely constructed Honduran cigars are made virtually entirely for the British market and are a cross between Cuban and Dominican cigars in terms of flavor. They are a quite powerful smoke with a nice spiciness to the flavor. They make an excellent after dinner smoke, particularly the larger sizes, and are a good alternative for those not wishing to pay premium prices for hand-made Havanas. Most come packed in bundles wrapped in cellophane, although some are conveniently available in nicely designed aluminum tubes.

Name	Length	Ring Gauge
No. 11	6¾	44
No. 13	5⅜	46
No. 14	5½	42
No. 16	5	42
No. 19 (Epicure)	4½	50
No. 20	4½	42
No. 17	4	42

Above and Right: The aluminum tube is packaging for a Don Ramos No. 19 Epicure, strong and very pleasant after dinner.

Dunhill

Rather like Davidoff, Dunhill also used to produce a great Cuban cigar until the Cuban government decided to take control of its cigar trademarking. This was incompatible with the way Dunhill was run, and so production switched to the Dominican Republic.

Unusually, Dunhill uses tobacco from a single year's crop to roll the cigars so they can be termed "vintage." The cigars are a medium-bodied smoke and are well constructed. Particular favorites are the Condados and Peravias, a corona extra and a churchill respectively.

Name	Length	Ring Gauge
Peravias	7	50
Fantinos	7	28
Diamantes	6⅝	42
Samanas	6½	38
Centenas (Pyramide)	6	50
Condados	6	48
Valverdes	5⁹⁄₁₆	42
Romanas	4½	50
Bavaros	4½	28

Above and Right: The Dunhill Valverdes—a well-constructed, medium-bodied smoke.

H. Upmann

In 1844 a European banker named Herman Upmann established this brand in Havana, Cuba. The Cuban variant come in a large selection of more than 30 sizes although some of these are machine made and should not be confused with the better quality hand-made versions.

Upmanns are also produced in the Dominican Republic, where they are particularly well made, the maker being Consolidated Cigars. Dominican Upmanns are a medium to mild smoke and use a lovely dark Cameroon wrapper leaf. Most of the Dominican cigars which have a Cuban counterpart are not available for purchase in Europe because of trademark regulations.

Name	Length	Ring Gauge
Dominican		
Corona Imperiales	7	46
Monarch Tubes	7	46
El Prado	7	36
Lonsdales	6⅝	42
Churchills	5⅝	46
Pequenos No. 100	4½	50
Robusto	4¾	50
Cuban		
Sir Winston	7	47
Monarch	7	47
Lonsdale	6½	42
No. 2 (Piramide)	6⅛	52
Corona	5½	42
Connoisseur No. 1	5	48
Petit Upmann	4½	36

Right: A 7in. Corona Imperiales.

La Gloria Cubana

This very well-constructed cigar is produced in Florida and the Dominican
Republic, the brand being owned by
one of the most knowledgeable men in
the trade—Ernesto Carillo. They represent exceedingly good value being one
of the best Dominican cigars on the
market for the least amount of money.

Like the Opus X, the Gloria Cubana
is a full-bodied cigar wrapped in a
beautiful dark leaf grown in Ecuador.
Production in the Miami factory was 1
million cigars in 1995 and the addition
of the factory in the Dominican
Republic will supply an additional 1.5
million cigars. Due to trademark laws,
they are not sold in the UK; there is
also a Cuban equivalent, which is now
not imported to Britain.

Name	Length	Ring Gauge
Soberano	8	52
Charlemagne	7¼	54
Churchill	7	50
Torpedo	6½	52
Wavell	5	50

*Above Right and Right: A box of Torpedo No. 1 cigars and
a single example of this Florida-made smoke.*

Licenciados

These good quality hand-made cigars have been available to buy since 1990. They are a classic style of Dominican cigar, which uses a pale-colored Connecticut-shadegrown wrapper.

There are just over 10 sizes in the range, with the gigantic Soberano at the top. This cigar is 8 ½in. long with a heavy 52 ring gauge. The cigars themselves are of excellent quality and give a mild smoke with a smooth flavor.

The band is very distinctive using a horsedrawn carriage as its logo. They are made by Matasa in the Dominincan Republic—who amongst other brands also manufacture the Romeo y Julieta cigars.

Name	Length	Ring Gauge
Soberano	8½	52
Presidente	8	50
Churchill	7	50
Excelente	6¾	43
Toro	6	50
Wavell	5	50
Wavell Maduro	5	50
Supreme Maduro	5	42

Right: This Licenciados Toro is 6in. long with a ring gauge of 50. It's a mild smoke with an excellent taste.

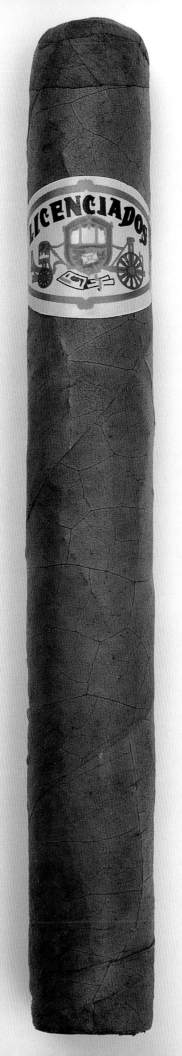

Macanudo

This brand, one of the best selling of all cigars in America, was originally founded in Jamaica in 1868 but are now produced in the Dominican Republic aswell, although the blend is the same for individual sizes regardless where they are produced.

There are several ranges of cigars within the brand and the most sought after are the Vintage Selction. These are made entirely in Jamaica using a Domincan filter and really are truly excellent cigars. They are reasonably full bodied with a delicious spicyness. In total, more than thirty sizes of Macanudo cigars are produced.

Name	Length	Ring Gauge
Vintage No. 1	7½	49
Vintage No. 2	6½	42
Vintage No. 3	5½	46
Vintage No. 4	4½	46
Vintage No. 5	5½	49
Vintage No. 6	7½	38
Prince Phillip	7½	49
Duke of Devon	5½	42
Hyde Park	5½	49

Right: A Macanudo Vintage 1993, a Jamaican-made cigar. Many Macanudos use Connecticut wrappers.

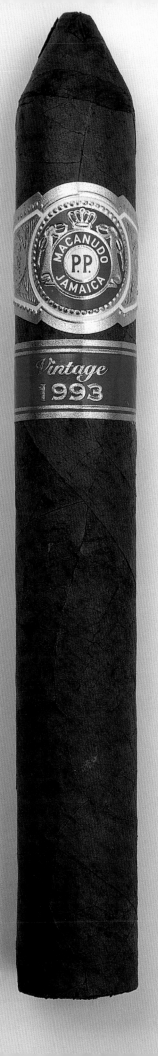

Montecristo

Montecristo is easily the most popular and widespread of all the Cuban brands. Half of all the cigars produced in Cuba are Montecristos, many of them being the petit corona sized No.4, the biggest selling Cuban cigar there is. The brand was introduced in 1935 and is named after the famous swashbuckling story the "Count of Montecristo" by Alexander Dumas.

Montecristo brand cigars are also made in the Dominican Republic by Jose Marti. Although much sought after, they are not produced in anywhere the same quantity as the Cuban version, and only seven different kinds are made.

Dominican Montecristos are medium strength, high quality cigars which are available in more-or-less the same sizes as the Cuban range with a couple of additions—a churchill and a robusto.

Cuban Montecristo cigars are similarly of a medium to full-bodied flavor. There are 11 different kinds to choose between. The No. 2 pyramide is one of the best-loved cigars in the world, giving an amazingly rich but smooth smoke. They are exceedingly popular and as such may be hard to find, but they are well worth hunting down and make a superb after dinner cigar, with their flavor developing the further and longer they are smoked.

Right: Dominican Montecristo No. 2, a 6in. smoke.

A mention must also go to the absolutely enormous Montecristo A. This monster of a cigar is 9¼in in length with a 47 ring gauge, it is currently Cuba's most expensive standard production cigar. This is definitely a cigar to relax with, as it provides a good three hours enjoyment.

Name	Length	Ring Gauge
Dominican		
Churchill	7	48
Corona Grande	5¼	46
Double Corona	6¼	50
No. 1	6½	44
No. 2	6	50
No. 3	5½	44
Robusto	4¾	50
Cuban		
A	9¼	47
No. 1	6½	42
No. 2	6⅛	52
No. 3	5½	42
No. 4	5	42
No. 5	4	40
Especiale	7½	38
Especiale No. 2	6	38
Joyita	4½	26

Above: The traditional Montecristo mark.

Right: Montecristo A—91/4in. of pure flavor.

Nat Sherman

In the United States, the name Nat Sherman is synonymous with very high quality smoking goods—both accessories and cigars, tobacco, and cigarettes. The present site of the main Nat Sherman New York store is 500 Fifth Avenue and is a paradise for cigar smokers.

Nat Sherman cigars are produced in several ranges, each with a different blend. There's the Gotham Selection which are fairly spicy to taste. and are named after addresses associated with Sherman heritage.

Then there is the Landmark selection, in which there are five sizes all named after famous buildings around New York. They are of medium strength with a hint of sweetness.

The City Desk Selection has four sizes. They are fairly large cigars and come wrapped in a dark Mexican madero wrapper; although they may appear to be full flavor cigars, they are in fact pleasantly mild.

The Exchange Selection has a Connecticut Shade wrapper and a blend of Dominican tobacco. Nat Sherman advertises this selection as "a cigar for latin lovers."

The Metropolitan Selection has five sizesall of which named after some of New York's gentlemens' clubs. The cigars themselves are fairly full flavored but are very smooth and very nicely balanced.

Right: From the City Desk Selection—a Dispatch.
This 61/2in. 46-gauge cigar has a Mexican maduro/oscuro wrapper and a great Dominican blend.

Other Nat Sherman cigar selections include the L.S.N., the V.I.P., the Host and the Manhattan, whose five cigars are the Gramercy, the Chelsea, the Tribeca, the Sutton, and the Beekman.

Name	Length	Ring Gauge
Gotham		
500	7	50
711	6	50
1400	6¼	44
65	6	36
City Desk		
Tribune	7½	50
Dispatch	6½	46
Gazette	6	42
Telegraph	6	50
Landmark		
Dakokta	7½	49
Algonquin	6¾	43
Metropole	6	34
Hampshire	5½	42
Vanderbilt	5	47
Metropolitan		
Anglers	5½	43
Nautical	7 (Piramide)	48
University	6	50
Explorers	5½ (Piramide)	50
Metropolitan	7 (Torpedo)	60
Host		
Hampton	7	50
Harrington	6	46
Hunter	6	43
Hamilton	5½	42
Hobart	5	50
Hudson	4⅞	32

Right: A 7in. Hampton from the Host Selection.

Partagas

As with most of the Cuban brands of cigars, there is a non-Cuban equivalent which is available to purchase in the U.S.

After the revolution in Cuba many of the rollers fled the country and set up business elsewhere. Due to complex trade-mark laws they were allowed to use the same brand name as their Cuban counterparts.

Cuban Partagas cigars are supremely well made, the Partagas factory in downtown Havana being probably the most famous of all cigar factories. They are very rich in taste and are available in a wide range of sizes of which the Series No. 4 and the Lusitania are the most sought after.

Dominican Partagas cigars are also of very high quality which is reflected in their premium prices. A popular cigar, they are mainly available in a nice colorado wrapper, from Cameroon, but also a madiro is available. The filler is Dominican or Mexican and the binder Mexican. There are about fourteen sizes, all of which are medium to full strength.

Name	Length	Ring Gauge
Dominican Republic		
No. 10	7½	49
8-9-8	6⅞	44
Royale	6¾	43
Maduro	6¼	48
Sabroso	5⅞	44
Naturales	5½	50
No. 4	5	38

Right: Partagas No. 6—a 6in., 34-gauge medium to full-flavored smoke.

Cuban

Lusitania	7⅝	49
Churchill DeLuxe	7	47
No. 1	6¾	43
8-9-8	6¾	43
Corona	5½	42
Series D No. 4	4⅞	50

Above: A No. 10, 7½in. 49-gauge.

Left: A Cuban 8-9-8 6¾in. 43 gauge cigar.

Punch

Punch is the second oldest cigar brand still in existence, being founded by Manuel Lopez in 1840. They were originally made with the British market firmly in mind and the name is taken from the satirical magazine of the same name: even today Mr Punch appears on the lid of each and every box.

Most of the sizes are produced in the La Corona factory in Old Havana and are of a medium strength and high quality construction. The most sought after sizes are the Double Corona and Punch Punch, but the Churchill is also an excellent smoke, particularly in the evening. As with other manufacturers there is also a parallel range of machine-made cigars. Sizes of the hand-made variants include:

Name	Length	Ring Gauge
Double Corona	7⅝	49
Churchill	7	47
Punch Punch	5⅝	46
Corona	5½	42
Petit Corona	5	42
Punchinello	4½	34
Tres Petit Corona	4¼	42
Petit Punch	4	40

Above and Right: Mr. Punch is immortalised on the label of the cigar boxes of the company founded by Don Manuel Lopez of J. Valley & Co. The cigar is a 7in. Churchill—an excellent evening cigar.

Romeo y Julieta

If someone has heard of a Cuban cigar but never tried one, this is the brand which is mentioned most often. It certainly has the most romantic name of any of the brands. The cigars were named after the tragic Shakespeare play and were originally intended for domestic use only: but soon they became popular over the world and at one time Romeo y Julieta was well known for producing over 20,000 different personalized labels for heads of state and other such important figures.

The cigars themselves are constructed of the highest possible quality and come in a large choice of more than 40 different sizes. Of medium flavor, these cigars have a sweetness about them that many find extremely palatable.

Name	Length	Ring Gauge
Churchill (tubed)	7	47
Prince of Wales	7	47
Cedros Deluxe 1	6½	42
Cedros Deluxe 2	5½	42
Cedros Deluxe 3	5	42
Belicosos	5½	52
Exhibicion No. 3	5½	46
Exhibicion No. 4	5	48
Corona	5½	42
Petit Corona	5	42
Tres Petit Corona	4½	40
Shakespeare	6⅞	28
Petit Julieta	4	30

Above: Romeo climbs to see his Juliet on the boxes of possibly the best-known cigar brand in the world.

Right: A Romeo y Julieta Churchill, a fine, long medium strength smoke.

MADE IN HABANA, CUBA

Santa Damiana

These cigars are made in the La Romana factory in the south-eastern part of the Dominican Republic. There are two ranges in this brand of cigar available, one for the American market and one for the United Kingdom and European markets. The cigars for the United Kingdom are imported by Hunters and Frankau Ltd, the sole importers and distributors of most Cuban cigars in the United Kingdom.

The European versions are richer in flavor than their American counterparts, reflecting the different styles of tastes in each market. The cigars are well-made, a very consistent smoke and use a light-colored Connecticut Shade wrapper.

Name	Length	Ring Gauge
Churchill	7	48
Corona	5½	42
Petit Corona	5	42
Panatela	4½	36
Robusto	5	50
Torpedo	6⅛	52

Right: The Torpedo is one of several new sizes of this brand recently been introduced. It is a pyramide, rich in flavor.

Trinidad

Trinidad is a name which conjures visions of smoking perfection in the eyes of a cigar connoisseur. It is the cigar which Castro himself uses for diplomatic gifts and cannot, as yet, be purchased.

However, a mid-1997 trade announcement said that Trinidads were to be sold on the open market. The cigar world waited with impatience and the brand was launched in early 1998. Many expected a cigar of exactly the same size as the one Castro uses — sadly this is not so.

In late 1997 an original box of 25 Trinidad cigars was sold for a new record of £9,980 — the purchaser must have been concerned when he heard that Trinidads were to be made more widely available; he can now rest safe in the knowledge that his investment is secured because of the difference in sizes!

Name	Length	Ring Gauge
Trinidad	7	38

Right: The Trinidad is soon to be launched to the public which will allow aficionados to obtain these rare, smooth smokes.

Valdrych

This is the most recently introduced Dominican cigar with a difference— they have been made specifically with the UK market in mind. They have a lovely powerful flavor and a dark wrapper leaf. The brand, owned by Maritza and Richard Ulrych, uses filler, binder, and wrapper not only from one country, but from one plantation. They are amongst the most flavorfull of all the non-Cuban cigars and are available in a good range of sizes.

Name	Length	Ring Gauge
Quisqueya Real	10	50
Monumento	8	50
Taino	6	50
Conde	4½	52
1904	6¾	46
Cabaillero	7¾	38
Fransisco	5½	46
Sublime	4	42

Above and Right: A box and individual example of the Taino.

RING
GAUGE GUIDE

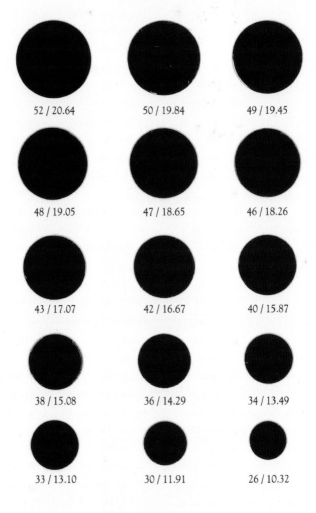

52 / 20.64	50 / 19.84	49 / 19.45
48 / 19.05	47 / 18.65	46 / 18.26
43 / 17.07	42 / 16.67	40 / 15.87
38 / 15.08	36 / 14.29	34 / 13.49
33 / 13.10	30 / 11.91	26 / 10.32

These holes are cut to the precise ring gauges of the most popular Havana sizes.

Please use them to guide your selection, but remember that they indicate the ring gauge of the cigar just after it left the maker's bench.

A cigar's shape may alter either in its packaging, particularly if it is "pressed" to a square shape, or according to the amout of moisture in it. So be careful not to force a cigar through a hole or you may damage its wrapper.

The numbers represent the diameter of the holes in 64ths of an inch i.e. 48 = 48/64th or 3/4 of an inch, or the equivalent in mm.